Letts EXPLORE

A View from the Bridge

ARTHUR MILLER

D0582985

Guide written by
Ron Simpson

A **Letts** Literature Guide

Extracts from A View from the Bridge © 1955 by Arthur Miller reprinted by kind permission of the author. A View from the Bridge is published in volume form by Penguin Books.

First published 1997

Letts Educational
Aldine House
Aldine Place
London W12 8AW
0181 740 2266

Text © Ron Simpson 1997

Typeset by Jordan Publishing Design

Text design Jonathan Barnard

Cover and text illustrations Hugh Marshall

Graphic illustration Hugh Marshall

Design © BPP (Letts Educational) Ltd

British Library Cataloguing in Publication Data
A CIP record for this book is available from the British Library

ISBN 1 85758 493 7

Printed and bound in Great Britain
by Nuffield Press, Abingdon

Letts Educational is the trading name of BPP (Letts Educational) Ltd

Contents

■ Plot synopsis

The events of the play occur in about 1950 in Red Hook, New York, in the shadow of Brooklyn Bridge. It is a poor community, consisting in large part of Italian immigrants, and relying for a livelihood on work at the docks. Alfieri, a lawyer who was himself born in Italy, is the audience's guide to the events in Red Hook as he tells the story of Eddie Carbone.

Eddie, a longshoreman, returns home to tell his wife Beatrice that her cousins (illegal immigrants) have arrived from Italy, earlier than expected. He in turn is shocked and upset by the news that his niece, Catherine, has been offered a job as a stenographer. When the immigrants, Marco and Rodolpho, arrive, Eddie finds Rodolpho's appearance and behaviour disturbing. Catherine, on the other hand, is attracted to him.

Some weeks pass before the next scene. During this time Rodolpho and Catherine's relationship has developed and Eddie fumes while waiting for them to return from the cinema. He gives two reasons for opposing the relationship: not only is Rodolpho 'weird', but he is seeking to gain American citizenship by marrying Catherine. Beatrice hints at another reason when she tells Catherine to be careful of the way she acts before Eddie.

After an unsuccessful meeting with Alfieri, Eddie deliberately provokes a confrontation, pretending to teach Rodolpho to box and imposing his power. Marco warns Eddie to leave his brother alone by asserting his strength in a chair-lifting competition.

Eddie is now so obsessed with keeping Rodolpho away from Catherine at all costs that he begins to act wildly and self-destructively. At Christmas, drunk, he comes on them together and kisses Catherine passionately and Rodolpho in violent mockery. The result, of course, is to confirm their plans to marry and make certain that Eddie loses Catherine.

At this point Eddie, after another failed talk with Alfieri, calls the Immigration Bureau. He wants Rodolpho out of the way and does not care who else suffers: Marco and two other illegal immigrants in the same block. Before the officers come, Beatrice finally talks frankly about Eddie's sexual failures. With the arrests, Eddie becomes an outcast, a traitor, and Marco publicly spits in his face.

Rodolpho and Catherine are to be married; he will become an American citizen. Before the wedding, however, Marco ignores the persuasion of Alfieri and the lovers and comes to challenge Eddie. In the fight Eddie draws a knife, the unarmed Marco turns the blade back into him and Eddie dies.

AMERICA

■ Who's who in
A View from the Bridge

Eddie

Eddie Carbone

Eddie is the tragic protagonist, meaning that he is the central character whom the tragedy befalls, but is he the tragic hero? Do you find anything heroic in Eddie? Alfieri says that he is pure – not purely good, but purely himself. Eddie has a code of honour, but breaks it to live by his obsession. As a student of the play, you need to determine just what this obsession is. He is Catherine's uncle and has undoubtedly behaved as a father and a friend to her, but what exactly does he feel towards her? There is no doubt that he has too much love, and that he wishes to be protective of her, but you need to consider how much his opposition to Rodolpho is due to a conviction that he is unsuitable and how much to sexual jealousy. Eddie is convinced that he is acting honourably, but he would not be the first person to misunderstand his own motives.

Eddie exists very much as part of a community and that gives him his strength and later brings his destruction. He is uneducated and hard-working, has a simple set of standards and a simple code of honour, and he knows that real men don't have blond hair and high voices. Real men also don't telephone immigration and, once he has lost his honour, his *name*, before the Liparis and others, Eddie is finished.

Beatrice

Beatrice

Beatrice is a simple and good woman whose problems seem incidental to the major tragedy of the play. Her problems are domestic and marital, but they are put aside as the Eddie/Catherine/Rodolpho/Marco tragedy works itself out. It is worth considering what Beatrice's problems are and whether they are her own fault in any way. Does

Beatrice accept too much? What could she have done to avert the situation? There are hints in the attempts she makes, always too late.

Beatrice becomes involved in events that are too much for her to deal with, in emotions too violent for her to possess, but what of her own standards, opinions and preferences? What are we told of them?

Beatrice seems at first to have potential as a comic character. Her confusions and panics over tablecloths and supper, plus her banter with her husband, are the stuff of many a television sit-com wife. But any hint of humour soon disappears: Beatrice's role is to suffer.

Catherine

Catherine

Catherine begins the play in all innocence; she is ready to accept people for what they appear to be, she sees no danger. She is dutiful and loving to her elders, she only thinks of taking a job because the principal advises it (and because she's the school's best pupil!), she happily waves at Louis despite Eddie's warnings. In many ways Catherine still acts like a little girl, but it is possible to find examples of her growing sexual maturity: look at evidence in her appearance and way of dressing. Even so, her first sight of Rodolpho brings wonder and delight. A crucial scene in her development is the progress from doubt to love at the beginning of Act 2.

The question that Arthur Miller makes us ask ourselves is: 'What makes such a sweet, obedient, trusting girl defy Eddie as she does?' There are many answers (the power of love, simply growing up), but you could consider what actions of Eddie's are responsible. To understand the development of Catherine's feelings, you should compare her outburst on pages 80 and 81 ('In the garbage he belongs!') with her last words in the play, as Eddie dies.

Marco

Marco

Of all the characters in the play, Marco is the one who is revealed most in his actions, least in his words. He is, like Eddie, driven by his belief in a code of behaviour, in traditional standards of right and wrong. In Marco's case, he follows the code purely and totally and, as a result, a respectable working man becomes a murderer. Arthur Miller deliberately lessens the guilt by beginning the fatal lunge with Eddie himself, but it is Marco who provokes the fight. What do you think drives Marco to this? The answer is not simply because Eddie has caused him to be deported, or any other practical reason.

Marco always acts correctly. To begin with, he is ready to act exactly as Eddie wishes: he is grateful to the Carbones and none of the issues that come up (such as Rodolpho singing) involve matters of honour. Marco's silence and correctness are a striking contrast to Rodolpho and he seems to have more in common with Eddie, but, when family honour is at stake, he has to assert himself in the chair incident.

In this strong, silent and dedicated character, Arthur Miller manages to create a killer whom we can see as good and honourable. This is helped by the fact that every passing reference shows the respect everyone has for Marco. Everything that he says has to do with something that really matters, practically or passionately: see if you can find any examples of unnecessary chat from Marco.

Rodolpho

Like most of the characters in the play, Rodolpho goes on a journey within himself. At the beginning, he is clearly immature and loves telling tall stories, making himself the centre of attention and treating American society like a typical youthful consumer. By the end he has taken responsibility for Catherine and, in a way, reversed roles with Marco, trying to persuade him to be sensible. Rodolpho will become an American, and already, he is less Italian than his brother: at the end he is the one who will settle for half and will accept blame simply to avert bloodshed.

The problem about Rodolpho's character is deciding if there is any truth in Eddie's criticisms. Eddie accuses him of not being normal, implying homosexuality. Of course, plenty of heterosexual men sing in high voices and can cook and sew, but Louis and Mike find him odd. Do we trust Louis' and Mike's opinion? What about the accusation of using Catherine as his passport to citizenship? To understand the relationship between the two, re-read the opening of Act 2: Catherine asks many of the questions we would like to ask.

Alfieri

We are told that Alfieri is in his fifties and lived in Italy until he was 25. We also find that he has certain views on the characters in the play: for instance, he loves Eddie more than his more sensible clients. But can we see him as a character himself? He has short scenes with Eddie and Marco, but his sensible talk means nothing to them. He is conventionally liberal, conventionally concerned. He is not a part of the drama, but he is the audience's link with the drama. His role is that of the chorus, as in a Greek tragedy, and is explained in the **Themes and techniques** section.

Tony, Louis, Mike, The Liparis

In *A View from the Bridge* there are five characters in tragic conflict and one commentator. There is also an unusual number of tiny parts, some of them non-speaking. These have no impact as individuals, but considerable importance as a group. Maintaining the code of society and keeping a good name before the world are crucial to people like Eddie and Marco, so the non-speaking Liparis matter. Eddie has betrayed their relatives as much as he has Beatrice's and their brief appearance marks him down as an outcast, just like Vinny Bolzano. Tony represents the syndicate, Louis and Mike are Eddie's neighbours and co-workers who share his prejudice against Rodolpho.

■ Themes and techniques in *A View from the Bridge*

Love

Love

Most of the characters' actions are brought about by love; it is love, not hatred, that fuels the violence. However, there are question marks over both the central loving relationships. Catherine has a great capacity for love and there is absolutely no doubt about her love for Rodolpho or her love (as a 'daughter') for Eddie. The opening section of Act 2 makes clear the strength of her emotions in both cases. The questions you need to answer are: what does she receive in return for so much love? Is Rodolpho as devoted to her as she is to him? What is the nature of Eddie's love?

Love is at the heart of Beatrice's problems: her love for Eddie is the main fixed point in her life, but increasingly is in conflict with her love for Catherine and, to an extent, her cousins. Even Marco's actions are originally dictated by love for wife and family: on his first arrival his love for his wife and gratitude that he will be able to help her are touchingly genuine.

Family

Family

Family loyalties are a major factor in the play: Beatrice to her cousins, Marco to his wife and to Rodolpho, the Liparis to their relatives. But there is also a more sinister aspect to the idea of 'family'.

These people are not just Italians, but Sicilians, as Alfieri makes clear at the very beginning. When he talks of gangsters in the same speech, the audience makes a connection and thinks of the Mafia. *A View from the Bridge* is not a play *about* the Mafia, but we need to appreciate this background to understand the play.

The Mafia is grouped in families, with, of course, godfathers. Among the major assumptions of the organisation is that the law is useless and direct 'justice' more effective. The Mafia is heavily involved in business as well as organised crime. 'Family' members are protected; enemies or those who betray the family are treated ruthlessly. You will find examples that reflect this world-view throughout the play. Right at the start, for instance, we find the mysterious 'they' who organise illegal immigration, bribe ships' captains and organise plenty of work for the immigrants until their debts are paid.

The concept of family in *A View from the Bridge* is thus menacing as well as conventionally comforting. In both its forms, it is central to the play.

Honour

Honour

Honour must be maintained; that is the inevitable consequence of the attitudes to family contained in this play. Insults to the family must be avenged; that is the basis of the vendetta, or blood–feud. So, as the play reaches its bloody climax, we have symbolic insults like spitting and repeated references to the need for apology. Honour must be maintained. One of the lesser reasons for Eddie's distaste for Rodolpho is that other workers laugh at him, an insult to Eddie and his family.

Apart from family honour, Arthur Miller always deals with personal honour: name and identity. John Proctor, in *The Crucible* (written two years before *A View from the Bridge*) refuses to sign his name to a dishonest document that could save his life, using the words, 'How may I live without my name?' Miller himself, told to betray possible Communists in the McCarthy-ite witch-hunt (see pages 54 and 55 of this guide), made a very similar response. The same code of honour applies here: Eddie, just before the fight, says 'I want my name, Marco', and the last few pages are full of significant repetition of names.

The law

Justice and the law

Justice and the law are not the same thing and the conflict between them runs through the play. The problem is increased by the fact that the first generation Americans of Red Hook do not really believe in the law, anyway. It is a master-stroke of Miller to give the chorus/narrator role to a lawyer and, within a few lines of the play opening, Alfieri is telling us of gangsters, the Sicilian past and a people unwillingly accepting the law. How little they accept it is, of course, immediately evident with the arrival of the illegal immigrants.

The law, then, can do no good and can even be used to do harm. Alfieri's attempts to explain the law to Eddie and Marco fail totally. Both are shocked and frustrated by the fact that what they see as justice cannot be carried out (against Rodolpho and Eddie, respectively) and also cannot relate this alien law to their traditional codes of honour. Marco even finds it 'a new idea' when Alfieri says it is not dishonourable to promise not to kill a man!

The danger with the law is that this community living by its own laws is within a city and a nation living by the orthodox laws. So Eddie has the power to step outside the laws of Red Hook, telephone the Immigration Bureau, triumph by the law of the land and perish by the laws of his community.

Chorus

The chorus

Arthur Miller saw this play in terms of a Greek tragedy. In the first incomplete draft of the play the title was *An Italian Tragedy* (an obvious hint at its origins) and the first completed version was in a one-act format. This enabled him to make the action continuous, drawing attention to the single line of plot which moved steadily towards the final tragedy and emphasising the inevitability of the ending. Despite the interval, a good production still makes us feel that inevitable and shocking progress. Greek tragedies observed the Unities: a single plot or story-line, a single setting and continuous time (or, at worst, a 24-hour time span).

Clearly Miller managed the first and (with some stretching) the second, but his plot had to unfold over months. How to make it continuous, but with a wide time-scale? He did this with clever use of the chorus. In Greek tragedy a group of anonymous citizens (identified as a group, not as individuals) informed the audience of events before the play, narrated off-stage happenings, commented on the characters, established norms of behaviour, told the audience what to think and even what was going to happen. Alfieri does all this and is thus able to chart the passing of time in his narration. Alfieri is, of course, a sort of super-chorus, with a name, a job, an age and a habit of hopeless intervention in the play, but we have as little interest in him as a person as if he was an anonymous citizen of Athens.

It is also interesting to consider whether other characters take some of the role of a Greek chorus. Do Louis, Mike and the Liparis have the same function as a chorus?

■ Text commentary

Act 1

Arthur Miller has divided the play into two acts: there are no separate scenes. In fact, he saw it as one continuous story, its continuity expressing a single tragic process. However, there are considerable gaps in time, so you will find it easier to examine the text in separate sections as well as in its complete form.

To assist you, this commentary presents the text in segments which emphasise the 'real' time scale. Throughout this guide page references are to the Penguin edition of A View from the Bridge/All My Sons.

Stage directions

The set remains unchanged throughout the play. It is what is known as a *composite* set; that is to say, it includes different elements within one unit. From this we learn that the action will take place in different areas. There is one dominant setting: Eddie's apartment. Eddie's living room is the only naturalistic piece of staging, complete with doors, furniture and so on. This places Eddie's family at the centre of the drama.

Family

However, the family is not the entire drama. The life of the community is also significant: the stairway and the telephone booth will become important in Act 2 and Alfieri's office will be the scene for two crucial scenes with Eddie. The set surrounding the apartment need not be realistic (note Miller's use of the word 'represents').

Two recent London productions opted, respectively, for a complicated and menacing apartment block and a bare setting with the living room raised up like a stage (or a boxing ring?)

The last stage directions before Alfieri enters tell us that two longshoremen are pitching coins and that a distant foghorn blows. What effect does Miller achieve by these words?

Alfieri's soliloquy (pages 11–13)

The role of Alfieri in the play

As we have seen, Alfieri has a choric function, performing the role of the

chorus in a Greek tragedy. To do this effectively he has to know a great deal about the characters and action, but he communicates with the audience (if anything) more effectively than with the other characters. Much of his speaking takes the form of *soliloquies*, in other words, 'talking alone' to the

Chorus   audience: here Louis and Mike are technically on stage, pitching coins, but Alfieri is isolated by the lighting.

You should be able to identify how Alfieri fulfils his choric role here: try to work out how he affects the audience's thinking on themes, characters and future events.

Italy and America

The characters are poised between being Italian and being American. Eddie's father came from Italy (doubtless his name is really 'Eduardo Carbone') and Beatrice has relatives in the homeland. Rodolpho sets about 'becoming an American' and Alfieri is an Italian who has been in the USA for maybe 30 years. Here he emphasises the Italian tradition.

Al Capone and Frankie Yale were famous gangsters of the 1920s, when

Alfieri had just arrived in America. At the end of the soliloquy, whilst admitting himself powerless, Alfieri refers back to Syracuse and Calabria. The reference to Al Capone as 'the greatest Carthaginian of all' also emphasises history. Carthage was an African city-state, the enemy of Rome; it is also the

The law   name of a town in Illinois, near to Chicago, Al Capone's base for his criminal activities. This shows that certain principles have not changed for centuries. How would you define those principles?

Mostly, of course, 'we settle for half'... but not always.

'Where you goin' all dressed up?': the family together (pages 13–25)

Eddie returns home from work with important news: his wife Beatrice's cousins have landed. They are illegal immigrants from Italy who were expected, but not so soon. Eddie's niece, Catherine, has news for him: she has been offered a job as a secretary even though she has not finished college. Eddie is surprisingly disturbed by this prospect.

The impact of this scene comes from the contrast between a family behaving normally and the air of menace that hangs over what should be normal tea-time activities. The scene is set for the inevitable tragedy. First we have

Alfieri's warnings, then the danger that lies in the illegal immigrants, finally the strangeness in Eddie and Catherine's relationship.

Family

And yet much of the *dialogue and humour* could be considered normal family behaviour. Analyse for yourself the signs of Catherine's affection, her desire to please and to help, the indications that Beatrice and Eddie have developed their relationship over a long time and the humour and teasing between people who know (and like) each other.

Hints of danger: the Vinny Bolzano story

When Eddie breaks the news of the arrival of B's cousins, all is happiness: Catherine claps her hands. Beatrice's state is described as 'unutterable joy'. But very soon comes the warning: 'if everybody keeps his mouth shut', all will be well: 'nothin' can happen'.

The law

Later, Eddie builds up the tension as the merest hint drives him to worry about the women not understanding the power of the United States Immigration Bureau. Finally, Eddie launches into the Vinny Bolzano story.

Eddie

This, of course, is a foretaste of Eddie's own story. As such, brief as it is ('Like Vinny Bolzano.... you can quicker get back a million dollars that was stole than a word that you gave away'), it is of major importance. It is Eddie who speaks the line that later applies to his own dishonour and the loss of his good name:

'How's he gonna show his face?' Ironically, Eddie finds it horrifying now.

Consider what it is that makes Vinny Bolzano's story so horrifying. After all, nobody dies, unlike the story we are watching, but there is no doubt of the impact of Vinny's tale. Why?

Honour

Eddie and Catherine: A tragic relationship

Already, at our first sight of them together, it is clear that Eddie's feelings for

Catherine

Catherine have tragic potential. We ought to consider from the start just what these emotions are. *A View from the Bridge* went through many versions before completion and, at first, Arthur Miller's main concern was (in his own words) with 'the mysterious world of incestuous feelings and their denial'.

Alfieri, our 'chorus', sums up Eddie very well near the end

of Act 1: 'We all love somebody, the wife, the kids – every man's got somebody that he loves, heh? But sometimes... there's too much. You know? There's too much, and it goes where it mustn't.' The stage direction when Eddie finally agrees to Catherine taking the job presents his feelings more sympathetically: 'with a sense of her childhood, her babyhood, and the years'.

Eddie

It is impossible to deny Eddie's incestuous sexual desire for Catherine, but equally it is unfair to him (and to Miller's subtlety as a playwright) to regard their relationship simply in this light. Eddie has in many ways been a good 'father' to her and, if you examine this section carefully, you will find many examples of her trust and confidence in him, and of his kindness towards her.

Before the news of Catherine's chance of a job, Eddie finds moments of tension in signs that she is growing up (her short skirt, high heels and 'walking wavy') or being too friendly to men (Louis). Is this just being protective? Does he want her to stay *his* little girl for ever?

Three points about their relationship that you might like to consider:

Which of the two more frequently touches the other affectionately?

What does it show about Eddie that he responds shyly to Catherine's greeting and is moved almost to tears by her 'madonna-like' appearance?

Do Eddie's objections to Catherine working in Nostrand Avenue have any basis in fact? Or is it just his fear of her growing up put into words?

Education: 'You'll never get nowheres unless you finish school'

Catherine is the best student in the class and Eddie wishes her to study further

Catherine

to better herself, but Eddie himself has received little or no education. Alfieri, the outsider, is of course the only character in the play with a university education. The people of Red Hook share the prejudices of the uneducated. It is ironic that education would have taken Catherine from Eddie, even if there had been no Rodolpho.

Family

Eddie, though, admires education. His first compliment to Catherine is 'You look like one of them girls that went to college'. Like a proud father, he wants the best for the next generation and has worked out that education is the way to escape from Brooklyn.

'You're the one is mad.'

Beatrice

By the end of this scene, the harmony has gone: even Beatrice (who has been unusually forceful in telling Eddie to let Catherine grow up) is out of sympathy with Eddie. Catherine is almost guilty and doing jobs with embarrassed eagerness. Beatrice turns away from Eddie, her chores an escape. As for Eddie, he sits staring at cigar smoke and checking his watch: there's more than one way in which time is passing quickly.

The arrival of the immigrants: 'Yes! I like sugar very much!' (pages 26–33)

Ten o'clock the same night: Marco and Rodolpho are brought to the house by Tony. There is much normal conversation comparing life in Italy and in Brooklyn, the prospects for work and so on. Rodolpho, however, proves a disturbing character with his blond hair and his high tenor voice.

Chorus

Note the introduction to this section.

Alfieri tells us that time has passed. He also, in three sentences, gives an ominous edge to this meeting. The vocabulary and sentence construction is almost Biblical in its dignity and simplicity: is there something Biblical about the story that is unfolding?

'She said they were poor!'

Honour

What is poverty? In the previous section Eddie, in a fine statement of the very principles of honour that he will betray, said '…suppose my father didn't come to this country, and I was starvin' like them over there… and I had people in America could keep me a couple of months? The man would be honoured to lend me a place to sleep.'

The people of Red Hook are poor; the people of Marco's village are starving. However, unlike Rodolpho (who immediately decides that he has rich relatives), Marco can see the truth.

Family

The presence of the wider 'family' is obvious here, though not particularly threatening. Tony is helpful, but clearly in charge. The importance of 'paying them off' will keep Marco and Rodolpho in work. As yet there are no problems, but their arrival owes as much to an illegal organisation as to relatives' generosity.

Marco

Marco will show himself powerful by his actions. His words are unfailingly

Marco

modest. Almost all his conversation is dominated by the wish not to cause trouble. He thanks people frequently, he quietens his younger brother, he refuses food, he wonders if they can accommodate him for the time being in such a small house, he sees the high (to him) wages as an opportunity to send money to his wife.

Family

The contrast with Marco makes Rodolpho seem even more unusual. Let us examine what is odd about Rodolpho, odd enough to produce the striking reactions that it does from Eddie and Catherine.

The paper doll: the pleasure principle

At first the only sign of difference in Rodolpho is his blond hair. Italians are

Rodolpho

supposed to be dark, but he claims that the Danes invaded Sicily. It is not until later that Eddie drops hints that it may be dyed. Rodolpho is young, immature and excited: is it surprising that he enjoys being the centre of attention? Perhaps his behaviour is rather trivial in the circumstances, but Catherine finds it charming.

Rodolpho is a performer: he laughs a lot; he tells a story with imagination and a sense of audience – note the *similes* (comparisons) in 'listening to the fountain *like birds*'/'The horses in our town are *skinnier than goats*'; he loves to exaggerate, as in the tales of the motorcycle and singing at the hotel; he sings *Paper Doll* (he is already half converted to American culture!) in a very high tenor voice. Like much popular music, this is a love song.

Love

You might think that Rodolpho is over-confident, conceited and thoughtless, but it is worth checking how he behaves towards Marco: he constantly seeks permission for his actions. Certainly his claims are excessive, almost absurd. 'I sing Napolidan, jazz, *bel canto*' is an extravagant boast: 'Napolidan' means folk songs from Naples and *bel canto* is the style of operatic arias. After all that, *Paper Doll* seems rather tame, but does Rodolpho's behaviour justify the reactions to it?

Eddie's reaction to *Paper Doll*

Eddie

On page 29 a stage direction, as so often in Miller's plays, is of great help to actor, producer and student alike: 'he is coming more and more to address Marco only'. From that point, examine the number and type of contributions that Eddie makes and you will find strong indications that he does not consider Rodolpho work talking to. Now examine what he says after *Paper Doll* (using stage directions as well) and decide why he reacts the way he does and whether what he says is reasonable. (Incidentally, his reference to 'Garbo' relates to Greta Garbo, a beautiful and mysterious film star of the 1930s.)

Catherine's response

Catherine

Is Catherine's response to Rodolpho any more balanced? She reacts to his blond hair as a miracle ('wondrously', says the stage direction), she finds his singing 'terrific' (she is 'enthralled', we are told) and she very quickly checks that he is not married.

Love

Is there anything in Catherine's background that makes her so ready to fall in love at first sight?

An interesting decision for the producer of this play is just how glamorous to make Rodolpho: Marco is clearly described as 'a square-built peasant of thirty-two', for Rodolpho we have (quite rightly) to rely on the varied opinions of other characters. Is he really a good singer, or is it just Catherine's love that makes it sound so wonderful?

Rodolpho

What is beyond doubt is that the tragedy is underway. Eddie's attempts to come between Rodolpho and Catherine are doomed. As the section ends, Rodolpho flatters her with a flirtatious confidence carried over from *Paper Doll*; she offers sugar and he accepts readily. The symbolism is none the worse for being obvious (they are 'sweet on one another') and Eddie's face is puffed with trouble.

Self-test questions (on pages 11–33)

Uncover the plot
Delete two of the three alternatives given, to find the correct plot. Beware possible misconceptions and muddles.

The play is set in Red Hook/Sicily/Calabria and is introduced by Alfieri, who is a longshoreman/immigration official/lawyer. From the beginning, he makes it clear that tragedy is inevitable/unlikely/possible. Eddie Carbone is delighted to see his daughter/niece/neighbour Catherine looking so beautiful, but the news that she has found a job makes him happy/furious/worried. He, too, has news: his/his wife's/Alfieri's cousins will arrive from Italy/Africa/Yugoslavia next week/tomorrow/at ten o'clock. They are illegal immigrants, so it is important not to speak to/betray/offend them. Eddie and Beatrice, his wife, welcome the cousins, Marco and Rodolpho, and are amazed at Rodolpho's blond/short/curly hair. Rodolpho/Marco/Eddie is strong and silent, but his brother tells stories about his singing/family/children and wishes to buy a house/a return ticket/a motorcycle. When he starts to sing, his voice is a baritone/a high tenor/a bass. Eddie is very pleased/troubled/bored at Catherine's attentive/rude/sisterly behaviour towards Rodolpho.

Who? What? Why? When? Where? How?
1 Who informed on his own uncle?
2 What did Rodolpho do in place of Andreola?
3 Why does Tony warn Marco and Rodolpho to be careful?
4 When does Marco hope to return to Italy?
5 Where is the firm that Catherine hopes to work for?
6 How does Eddie know that the immigrants will get plenty of work?

Who said... about whom?
1 'He sang too loud.'
2 'Very nice man.'
3 '...(he) was learning his trade on these pavements…'
4 'They got stool pigeons all over this neighbourhood…'
5 'You're the madonna type.'
6 'He trusts his wife.'

Open quotes
Find and complete the following:
1 'And now we are quite civilised... '
2 'The horses in our town are... '
3 '...she's seventeen years old... '
4 '...you can quicker get back a million dollars that was stole than... '
5 'My wife – she feeds them…'
6 'He was as good a man as he had to be…'

Prove it!
Find evidence in the text to prove the following statements:
1 The Italian community in Red Hook does not trust the law.
2 Family loyalty is all-important.
3 Rodolpho's stories are over-imaginative.

'You're a woman, that's all, and you got a nice boy' (pages 33–45)

Two weeks later: Eddie and Beatrice are waiting for Catherine and Rodolpho to return from the Paramount Cinema. Eddie gets in conversation with Louis and Mike: the topic of conversation is of course Rodolpho, a trouble to Eddie, a joke to the others. When the young lovers return, Rodolpho goes for a walk. Eddie upsets Catherine and himself by arguing that Rodolpho is using her to gain his American passport, while Beatrice urges Catherine to break with Eddie.

Eddie Carbone has a destiny

Chorus

Eddie

Before the lovers return from the cinema, an extended choric section lets the audience see how deep-rooted are the troubles that have come to the Carbones in two weeks.

In a five-line speech of Alfieri's, Eddie changes in many ways: time has passed, his stage position is different, but above all he has gained a destiny. A course of action is mapped out for him, that he must follow. In Alfieri's speech, note how cleverly Miller tells us that an ordinary man can be a tragic protagonist: it is not essential to be a king, a general or a great lover. Eddie expected to spend his life working, eating, going bowling; now he has to work out his destiny.

Nice kid, or weird?

The situation regarding Rodolpho has developed in the two weeks since he

Rodolpho

Family

arrived. Arthur Miller now uses the composite set to move easily from the house doorway to the street to inside the house. With one important exception, all the conversation is about Rodolpho and, in the way it tells the audience what has happened and offers alternative views on events, it complements Alfieri's choric function.

In conversation with Beatrice, Eddie's main worry is not that Rodolpho is looking for a passport, though he does mention the problem of his 'advertising himself' (so risking capture) and worries that 'he's taking her for a ride'. What really troubles Eddie is that Rodolpho is 'weird'. Examine the build-up from his worrying about their late return (at 8 o'clock!) through sentences like 'He gives me the heeby-jeebies' and obsessive ravings about Rodolpho's blond hair and his singing, to the conclusive statement: 'For that character I didn't bring her up'.

Eddie's views on Rodolpho do not change between his conversation with Beatrice and the one he has outside with Louis and Mike, but his role in the conversation does. No longer is he the one leading the criticism; now he is embarrassed to receive it.

Compare Eddie's view of Rodolpho with those of Louis and Mike. Is Eddie affected by their views?

Marco

Rodolpho is 'funny'. What does 'funny' mean here: 'funny peculiar' or 'funny ha-ha'? Note the word-games that Miller plays with 'funny', 'sense of humour' and so on.

What are everyone's impressions of Marco, now that he has been in Brooklyn for two weeks? Is there some irony in these impressions, considering Marco's later role in the drama?

'I got other worries'

Beatrice

The attention moves away from Rodolpho only briefly, when Beatrice responds to Eddie's increasing demands that she should worry about Catherine's love affair. 'Everything is great with you,' Eddie claims, and Beatrice briefly expresses her worries – briefly, because Eddie refuses to listen. Sexual relations have broken down – not, as Eddie says, because of worries about the 'submarines', but for many weeks before that.

Love

Very little is said. What is all-important is that this is placed in the middle of a conversation in which Eddie is trying to argue against Catherine's romance (or marriage?)

Why does he object:

because Rodolpho is 'weird';

because he thinks Rodolpho is after a passport;

because his desire for Catherine is such that he is unable to be a husband to Beatrice;

or even, as Beatrice suggests, because he cannot accept Catherine growing up ('What're you gonna stand over her till she's forty?')

Lovers and family

The lovers return happily, Catherine excited (by the film, she says), Rodolpho eager to see Broadway (but very polite in asking). Both are amused by the differences between Italy and Brooklyn (no fountains, no orange trees), but Rodolpho gets no response to his attempts at familiarity. He is sensitive and subtle enough to go for a walk and once again becomes a topic for conversation, not a character on stage. Once again we see him through others' eyes. Which is the real Rodolpho?

Love

Catherine must decide

Catherine need not yet choose between Eddie and Rodolpho, but already she must make important decisions. Is she to continue to believe the man whom she has trusted all her life? Can she prepare herself to say goodbye to Eddie? The girl who shouts 'I don't believe it' at Eddie finds herself, at the end of this section, 'at the edge of tears, as though a familiar world had shattered'.

Catherine

Duologues

You are familiar, of course, with the word 'dialogue' – speech involving more than one person. *Duologue* has a similar meaning, except that the conversation is specifically between two people. This section is made up almost entirely of duologues, beginning with Eddie and Beatrice, though there is the short Eddie/Louis/ Mike dialogue. Note how the duologue format is maintained when the lovers enter.

Louis and Mike leave as Catherine and Rodolpho enter. There are three on stage, but Rodolpho soon leaves.

Eddie's duologue with Catherine builds to a climax; she rushes into the house. After two short explosive lines, Eddie leaves the house. Once again, a duologue ensues: Beatrice and Catherine.

Consider what the advantages of a duologue are over a scene involving several people. The duologue may lack variety, but what does it gain?

Catherine and Eddie

Eddie wants to resume the relationship he has had with Catherine: what is, at least on the surface, a friendly family relationship. Hence the attempts at smiles – and, on Catherine's side, the friendly arm-punch. We all know the

situation where we try to keep a conversation on a safe subject, but our real feelings (of envy, jealousy or worry, perhaps) force us into using the wrong words.

Eddie is obsessed by his love and his destiny: how much more difficult is it for him to keep to the conversation he wants to? Look at the way he presents Catherine's failings: 'I

Family

bless you and you don't talk to me', 'I don't see you no more' and other similar statements. What does this suggest about Eddie's feelings and how he feels Catherine has let him down? What has Catherine done to justify this?

Love

Over-riding Catherine's protests and excuses, Eddie lets his obsession burst out in ever more violent form: from saying Rodolpho should ask permission, to the passport accusation, to descriptions of Rodolpho as a hit-and-run guy involved in a racket (Mafia hints?) to the final, simple declaration: 'the guy is no good!'

You might like to think how much evidence there is for what Eddie says about Rodolpho. You might also like to examine the speech on page 41 beginning 'You don't think so!' as the words of a man out of control.

Beatrice and Catherine

The key words in this duologue are 'baby', 'little girl' and 'grown woman'. Catherine is not guilty in any real sense of the word, but Beatrice makes it clear that she has helped to foster Eddie's feelings for her, not deliberately, but by her girlish affection.

Family

When Catherine walks around in front of Eddie in her slip or talks to him when he is in the bathroom in his underwear, it is the act of an innocent who sees him as a 'father', but it helps to inspire guilty feelings in Eddie. You will have noticed how reluctant Catherine is to do anything to hurt Eddie: the 'happy families' situation which means so much to him has been real. Despite the upset he has caused over Rodolpho, she still says, 'It just seems wrong if he's against it so much'.

Catherine

What Beatrice says now is unfailingly right. The message is that Catherine is a grown woman and must act like one. She does not need to fight Eddie, but her future is with Rodolpho. Where Beatrice is at fault is in leaving this excellent advice till too late: she has tried, but failed, twice before. What can Beatrice do now? Very little, maybe nothing. What could Beatrice have done in the months before Marco and Rodolpho arrived? That is her contribution to the tragedy.

Jealousy and love

Love

Sadly, jealousy frequently accompanies love. It is interesting to compare two references to jealousy in this section and consider the characters' reactions. Look at page 34 ('Ah, go on, you're just jealous') and page 44 ('he thinks... maybe I'm jealous...'). What do these two instances show about the characters involved?

Alfieri and Eddie: 'I don't quite understand what I can do for you...' (pages 45–50)

For the first time Alfieri plays a part in the action, or rather, fails to play a part. Eddie comes to him, explaining his fears and frustrations, his sense of destiny, and hoping that the law can take the burden from him. Alfieri repeatedly explains that there is nothing the law can do and, as he fails Eddie, he and the audience become increasingly aware that tragedy is imminent.

The problem

Family

It is in this scene that the certainty of coming horror grips the audience. Pause before considering it to remind yourself of the problem. There is a crime here, but it is not the crime that is destroying the characters. After all, Eddie and Rodolpho are on the same side (*so far*) in the matter of illegal immigration. In the last scene Beatrice burst out 'with open fright and fury'; Eddie walked out of the house 'in guilt'; Catherine finished the scene 'with some fear, with a discovery... as though a familiar world had shattered'. Rodolpho provokes violent reactions and there is a fifth piece to the jigsaw, not seen since his arrival. What can Alfieri do?

Alfieri

Chorus

Although Alfieri takes part in this section as a normal character, he does not abandon his chorus role. He introduces Eddie with a brief speech and links up to the next section with another of his soliloquies. His certainty of disaster communicates itself to the audience. Notice, in his first speech, the way in which Eddie's destiny has already taken him over: it is as though he has already committed the crime, he is filled with guilt and revenge. A striking simile here is 'His eyes were *like tunnels*'. It is the sort of phrase that offers many different meanings. Form your opinion and then compare it with those of others. They will vary, but menace will be present in all of them.

The speech that leads to the next stage of the action (pages 49–50) is worth careful study, as the perfect definition of the inevitability of tragedy. Tragedy on stage (notably, though by no means only, Greek tragedy) depends on the audience's knowledge that these things will certainly happen and that witnessing them becomes a purging of the emotions, almost a ceremony. The wise old woman here reminds us that the Gods looked down on Greek tragedy.

Now ask yourself: why is this tragedy inevitable?

'I'm only a lawyer'

Alfieri's first speech to Eddie begins, 'I don't quite understand what I can do

The law

for you. Is there a question of law somewhere?' If you examine what Alfieri says to Eddie throughout this scene, you will find these ideas repeated again and again. Alfieri's key words are 'law', 'legal(ly)', 'proof/provable' and 'nothing' (as in nothing to be done). Eddie, on the other hand, uses such phrases as 'I know', 'I see', 'I mean', and 'Right?' (in the sense of confirming agreement). They are talking two different types of evidence and there is no way that the law can solve Eddie's problem. Alfieri is not unsympathetic and gives Eddie some good advice (the same as Beatrice gave him), but his message that there is no law for what Eddie is thinking about shocks Eddie and forces him to seek his own solution.

'The guy ain't right'

You can undoubtedly think of several reasons why Eddie so often changes his

Rodolpho

objections to the Rodolpho/Catherine relationship. In part, though, it simply depends on the fact that he is not articulate enough to put over the ideas he feels, so he simply describes Rodolpho as 'weird'. Here he goes further than he has done so far in specifying Rodolpho's effeminacy.

In 1956, when the first London production of *A View from the Bridge* was due to open, the Lord Chamberlain, the censor at that time, banned the play. His decision was based on the grounds of the depiction of homosexuality on stage, not incest (which is, of course, a more central theme). The producers saved the production by converting the Comedy Theatre into a private club for the run of the play!

Now Eddie struggles, in speeches that grow longer as his furious obsession drags out every last detail that is troubling him, to explain that Rodolpho 'ain't right'. Starting with his blond hair and slight build, he moves on to his high tenor voice, dressmaking skills and angelic appearance.

Do you find any of these convincing? And would you agree that many of these reveal more of Eddie than of Rodolpho? What sort of a man condemns dressmaking as unfit for men?

What would Eddie think of a man who (like himself) talks of kissing another man who is sweet and angelic – and eventually does so?

Eddie Carbone is very mixed up, but it is still clear to him that he must not lose face in front of his fellow-workers: 'Paper Doll/Blondie' is a liability.

Alfieri's advice

Alfieri does not wish to be unhelpful, but the law cannot do anything, Whilst insisting that he cannot help, he gives two pieces of advice. As a lawyer, he feels compelled to mention the one course of action with which the law can offer some help to Eddie.

The law

Love

'There's only one legal question here,' he says, and he and Eddie know that neither wants to do anything about the illegal entry. However, the idea is planted in Eddie's mind.

The second piece of advice is good, if only Eddie could accept it. There are three crucial speeches from Alfieri on pages 48 and 49: 'You know, sometimes God mixes up the people' presents the clearest summary of Eddie from a sympathetic point of view. 'The child has to grow up and go away...' echoes Beatrice's earlier words: 'You're a woman, that's all... and now the time came when you said good-bye'. On the next page, he puts it less charitably: 'She can't marry you, can she?' Eddie, predictably, is furious at this.

Sympathy for Eddie? The punk and the patsy

We have no sympathy for Eddie's views on Rodolpho or his attempts to bring the law to bear on him. Do we, though, have any sympathy for the sobbing, helpless man who is convinced that his little girl has just been stolen from him?

Eddie

Re-read Eddie's long speech beginning 'What can I do?' and decide if he has a case.

You may be used to a different type of 'punk' – it is a word that has constantly changed its meaning. In Elizabethan times it meant a prostitute; here it is a generalised term for a no-good, worthless individual. A 'patsy', of course, is a fall-guy, the victim of others' sharp practice.

A Trial of strength: Marco and Eddie (pages 50–58)

All are in the house after dinner. Most of the conversation is apparently harmless and trivial. After a time, however, Eddie raises the topic of Catherine and Rodolpho and works himself into a state of subdued ferocity. He suggests that Rodolpho might like to spar with him and learn how to box. After a short while, he staggers Rodolpho with a blow. Marco then offers him a trial of strength, lifting a chair. Eddie fails, Marco succeeds.

Symbolism

By using *symbols* authors can make one thing represent another, often more important or powerful. Objects can symbolise ideas and people can be symbolised by details. Here, in this last section of Act 1, most of the acts are symbolic, a power struggle being described in apparently harmless acts and words.

Almost nothing happens, yet this is the fitting climax to an act in which we have seen hints of desperate tragedy. There is an apparently light-hearted conversation, with Beatrice even reverting to the dizzy sit-com character of happier days ('I didn't know they're sardines!') After some discussion of life in an Italian village, Eddie launches into an attack on Rodolpho's courtship of Catherine, but his language is now more moderate. Marco accepts his rulings and everything subsides. The young people dance to a new record. Eddie controls himself before his character assassination of Rodolpho goes too far and then the party settles down to some gentle horse-play: sparring, dancing and weight-lifting.

Honour

That is what happens on the surface; what is symbolised is full of menace and meaning.

Life on the boats and in the village

Eddie is restrained at first, but every word and gesture represents his refusal

to accept Rodolpho in the happy family setting. When Catherine mentions that the men went to Africa, Eddie gives a significant glance and she defends herself: 'It's true, Eddie'. What is the meaning of that glance? Certainly the meaning of his next few speeches is clear enough: every one is pointedly addressed to Marco and the moment Rodolpho speaks, Eddie rounds on him. Marco talks about his wife and Eddie listens patiently until Rodolpho joins in, whereupon Eddie makes a crude comment about unfaithful wives and 'a couple extra' kids. To Eddie, Rodolpho symbolises a woman-stealer; his comment follows instinctively.

Family

'It ain't so free here either'

'It's more strict in our town', says Rodolpho, explaining the absence of unexpected children. Eddie is thus given an excuse to explain that Rodolpho is behaving wrongly towards Catherine – if 'explain' is the right word for such a grinding out of prejudices. Note how he speaks in the third person ('I seen greenhorns sometimes get in trouble that way'), pretending he is discussing a general situation, but makes his meaning so clear that both Rodolpho and Beatrice respond by referring to Rodolpho. So far there is no open hostility: Eddie holds back his anger and constantly checks that Marco understands and agrees with him.

Love

Marco

Most interesting is the response of Marco to Eddie's thinly disguised comments. Examine what he says on pages 53 and 54 ('No, Beatrice, if he does wrong you must tell him' to 'That's why we came') and consider what Marco's feelings are at this time and his reasons for speaking as he does.

Eddie's motivation

As so often in Arthur Miller's plays, the stage directions are the key to much

Eddie

understanding. Essential to a great performance in a Miller play is the ability to reveal what is beneath the surface of the character. Here we may ask ourselves whether Eddie wishes to behave so appallingly, or whether he simply cannot avoid it. Read through the stage directions relating to Eddie from when he goes to his rocking chair (page 54) to asking Marco about boxing (page 56). Apart from his words (about Rodolpho's 'feminine' qualities), his looks and movements reveal a man in the grip of an obsession.

Conscious symbols

From the point when Catherine puts on a record to dance to, almost every

Catherine

act is chosen by the character to bear an extra meaning. This is an important moment for Catherine, who has always wished not to hurt Eddie. Much as she enjoys dancing with Rodolpho, that is not the reason for doing it or for choosing this record, *Paper Doll*. What do you think dancing to *Paper Doll* symbolises to Catherine? Again, the clue is in the stage directions.

Rodolpho

Eddie mounts his next attack verbally and the symbolism is obvious. He is pretending to say that singing, cooking and making dresses open up opportunities for Rodolpho; he means that they are signs of his effeminacy.

Look carefully at Eddie's behaviour in the boxing lesson. Firstly, it is a less unlikely way to behave than we might think; 'the fights' were a regular entertainment for working men and many escaped from the docks or the factories by their boxing talent. Eddie is more friendly to Rodolpho and speaks to him by name (a rarity for Eddie) and by nickname ('Danish', for his blond hair). He does not really hurt Rodolpho and avoids humiliating comments. All the points he is making are symbolic, not real. Consider what the symbolic implications of the sparring session are: they are far more than simply, 'I'm tougher than you are'.

Family

Rodolpho

Marco responds at last: family loyalty is greater than his concern not to irritate his benefactor, Eddie, but the first symbolic response comes from Rodolpho. He denies that Eddie hurt him ('with a certain gleam and a smile') and then calmly moves to his own act of defiance. When Catherine asked him to dance before, he tried to refuse, 'in deference to Eddie'. Now he invites her to dance and the song is still *Paper Doll*.

Symbolically, he is saying that the 'paper doll' is going to stand up for himself and that Eddie will achieve nothing but defiance by his bullying. As the 'paper doll' is a symbol of Rodolpho, so the dancing to the song shows that he is more than just a paper doll. If any doubt remains that Eddie has lost control of the situation, Marco's triumph with the chair symbolises family solidarity, strength, rejection of Eddie's bullying and ultimately, triumph.

So, four of the five main characters have revealed their positions and attitudes at the end of Act 1 by a symbolic act:

Catherine by dancing to *Paper Doll* on the phonograph (record player);
Eddie by challenging Rodolpho to spar;
Rodolpho by resuming the dance;
Marco by challenging Eddie to lift the chair.

Beatrice

Only Beatrice lacks such a defining moment. Why? You can find the answer in her words and actions throughout the last few minutes of the act. Here are some examples to help you make up your mind:

'Go ahead, Rodolpho. He's a good boxer, he could teach you';

'He's very good!' (she senses only the comradeship in it now).

To the interval

Compared with, for example, Shakespeare, most modern playwrights have the chance to exercise detailed influence over productions of their plays. Think of as many production features as you can which are written down in Miller's text, but not mentioned in a Shakespeare play. The director is, in a sense, invited to re-interpret Shakespeare, whereas there is a much more precise production blueprint with contemporary playwrights such as Miller.

One such element is the interval. In Shakespeare, five acts do not mean four intervals, so the placing of the interval(s) is a matter for the producer. But why does Miller send the audience out for a rest at this point? What does he want us to think about? What do you anticipate in Act 2?

One interesting point to think about in the interval: compare the behaviour of the family together in the scene when the immigrants arrive and in the final scene of Act 1. Concentrate on all five people, not just Eddie, and examine their relationships. Then ask yourself: has the centre of the family shifted?

The law

Self-test questions (on pages 33–58)

Uncover the plot
Delete two of the three alternatives given, to find the correct plot. Beware possible misconceptions and muddles.

Eddie waits for Catherine and Rodolpho to return from a dance/the cinema/work. He is worried about their relationship, because he regards Rodolpho as poor/lazy/effeminate. His opinion is supported /mocked/ignored by Louis and Mike. When Catherine returns, Eddie emphasises a different concern: that Rodolpho is using her to gain more work/money/his passport. Catherine then talks to Beatrice, whose advice is to behave in a more friendly/aggressive/adult manner to Eddie. Beatrice attacks/encourages/ignores Catherine's relationship with Rodolpho. Eddie seeks help from Beatrice/Alfieri/Marco, but is told that the only concern of the law in this case is justice/family feuds/illegal immigration. Eddie is furious/disappointed/amused when Alfieri points out that Catherine cannot marry him. In the house, Catherine defies/pleases/shocks Eddie by dancing with Rodolpho. Eddie then attempts to affirm his manhood/skill/experience by sparring with Rodolpho, but Marco responds by successfully challenging Eddie to a fight/a work-out/a trial of strength.

Who? What? Why? When? Where? How?
1 Who go bowling together in Flatbush Avenue?
2 What did Rodolpho do with Catherine's old dress?
3 Why did Rodolpho refuse to dance with Catherine at first?
4 When did Eddie work in Hoboken, Staten Island, the West Side and Jersey?
5 Where did Alfieri go to try to get advice and help with Eddie's problem?
6 How does Brooklyn surprise Rodolpho?

Who said... about whom?
1 '...he's a regular bull.'
2 'His eyes were like tunnels'
3 'You think I'm jealous of you, honey?'
4 '...if he's here for a good time, then he could fool around!'
5 '...a son-of-a-bitch punk like that – which he came out of nowhere!'
6 'You're like a father to him!' (two people)

Open quotes
Find and complete the following:
1 'Well, he ain't exackly funny, but...'
2 'Girls don't have to wear black dress...'
3 '...there is too much love for the daughter...'
4 'But if you act like a baby and he...'
5 'And with that wacky hair; he's like...'
6 'It's almost three months...'

Act 2

Christmas: Catherine chooses Rodolpho (pages 59–65)

Circumstances make possible the crucial confrontation. Rodolpho has not been hired to work at the docks and takes advantage of this to spend the day at home with Catherine. She is working at dressmaking; he is eager to consummate their relationship sexually. They discuss various matters (most importantly, whether they could live together in Italy), but are moving towards the bedroom when Eddie arrives. He is very drunk; a case of whisky slipped from a net at work. In a brief, violent scene Eddie kisses both of them (with different implications) and tells Rodolpho to leave; Catherine and Rodolpho state publicly their intention to marry.

Time and place

Dates and times are approximate in Act 1; we are seldom given the e precistime–relationship between different scenes. Act 2 is different. The chorus makes an announcement, setting the scene precisely for the important events that are imminent. The date is December 23rd; the whisky is Scotch; the pier it was being unloaded at is No. 41;

Chorus   the weather is cold, without snow. For these momentous events, we must have precise indications. This is a formal announcement, although Alfieri slips in a personal note at the end referring to his later conversation with Catherine. Why do you think Alfieri refers to Rodolpho as 'the boy'?

The precise dating continues in Act 2: on December 27th, just after 6 o'clock, Eddie visits Alfieri and rings Immigration. The final tragedy takes place on the following Saturday. Unlike Act 1, Act 2 has the audience metaphorically reaching for a calendar as the action accelerates.

Rodolpho: 'I show you what I be!'

Rodolpho has changed; or is it just that we have never seen him alone with

Rodolpho

Catherine before? He speaks with a new confidence and maturity. The opening of the act tells us, with astonishing economy, how different he is from what Eddie thinks, or even how Alfieri refers to him: 'the boy'. As the lights rise, he is watching Catherine arrange a paper pattern (not dressmaking himself?) Immediately and concisely, he expresses his desire for Catherine: he is hungry for her love, either immediately (as nearly happens shortly afterwards) or in a speedy marriage (as his next lines suggests).

Love

'I have nearly three hundred dollars': for the marriage, certainly, but it also indicates that Rodolpho has been working for some time and has been saving sensibly. You should make a comparison with what Eddie said he was doing with his money and find some lines in Act 1 which Rodolpho has proved to be wrong.

Catherine

Now compare Rodolpho with Catherine. Throughout Act 1 he has been the 'kid', the impetuously naive one for whom allowances have to be made. In this scene he is the more mature one, coaxing Catherine to share his maturity of attitude and emotion. Catherine, at one point, even says 'don't laugh at me!' when *he* finds *her* naive: this, the man who everybody only needed to look at to burst out laughing! See how many other examples you can find of Rodolpho speaking to Catherine as though she is much younger than he.

Rodolpho the American

The question of language is intriguing in this play. Of course, the fact that

Rodolpho

most of the characters are uneducated and possibly were brought up speaking Italian means that there is no need for a huge contrast between the speech of the Italians and that of the Americans. Marco is very silent in any case, and, on their first arrival, a few inversions ('Thousand–lire notes they threw from the tables') give a slight sense of the foreign in Rodolpho.

Now that he is at home in the country and with the language, Rodolpho's imaginative personality bursts out in poetic language: the gentle romance of 'If I take in my hands a little bird...'; the intense *metaphor* (an implied comparison) of 'I would be a criminal stealing your face'; the pride and passion of the repeated questions: 'Do you think I am so desperate?' He may not be an American yet, but how eloquent he is in the Americans' language!

Italy and America

This is the test question that Eddie has told Catherine to ask Rodolpho: Can we live in Italy when we are married? An affirmative answer would show that he really loves her, that he is not just looking for citizenship. But would it? Would it show her that he really loved her if he took her to a country he himself has been unable to survive in?

Love

Rodolpho gives a much better answer, which is worth reading again in the speeches beginning 'There's nothing!', 'No; I will not marry you to live in Italy' and 'I am furious!' In these you can see Rodolpho's pride in himself and in his country and his loving responsibility as a husband.

Catherine: 'I'm not a baby, I know a lot more than people think I know'

Catherine seems immature and inarticulate compared to Rodolpho, but is that

Catherine

a fair assessment? Her talk of living in Italy is all rather foolish; she thinks Rodolpho could go to Rome and sing (on the strength of one night deputising for Andreola!) and that there *must* be jobs somewhere (despite everything Marco and Rodolpho have said), but are her motives so foolish? Maybe she just wants Rodolpho to say the word (that she matters more than a passport) and they can stay in Brooklyn. Or there is a more sinister reason?

Catherine says 'I'm afraid of Eddie here.' She is shrewd enough to see that Eddie could ruin their marriage, while at the same time being generous enough to admit what he has done for her. She is cunning enough to know that Eddie can be deceived ('Tell him you'd live in Italy – just tell him') and loving enough to want him to be happy. In the speeches from 'It's only that I...' to 'I don't know why I have to do that, I mean.' (page 62), Catherine expresses the depth of her love for Eddie at the moment that she knows she must give it up – and that is why she weeps.

Love

Explore the sort of language used by Catherine here (the broken sentences, the simple phrases, the girlish slang). It is quite different from the poetry of Rodolpho, but they get to the same place ('I love you, Rodolpho'/'If I take in my hands a little bird... I will not let her out of my hands because I love her so much'). Catherine's 'I don't know anything' at least shows self-knowledge.

Beatrice: Catherine's view

Things are never quite as straightforward as they appear in the world of Arthur Miller's plays. Catherine, the innocent, suddenly reminds us with

Beatrice

unexpected shrewdness that it is naive to think of Eddie as a villain, Beatrice as a long-suffering saint, etc. Re-read the 'Then why don't she be a woman?' speech and penetrate beneath the childish vocabulary to an interesting alternative view of the Carbone marriage.

Contrasts

Rodolpho and Catherine gradually shed their excess emotional baggage (his anger at the accusations, her grief about Eddie and so on) and move together in a mood of gentle inevitability. 'And don't cry any more' means forever. Everything moves into security and fulfilment.

At this point, Eddie enters. Note how completely the mood changes.

Eddie

Lights go up in the street; the loving security of the bedroom is broken into. Eddie is loud and staggering. Above all, note how Miller deliberately overdoes the whisky: three bottles in different pockets. Eddie has taken his share of the cargo for Christmas, of course, but the impression is of a man who has been drinking enough for three.

'Don't make me do nuttin''

Considering that these are physical and passionate people, their violent emotions have not yet led to violent action: even the boxing match was more symbolic than a real contest. At the end of this short section, Eddie knows that he cannot now avoid violent action unless Catherine and Rodolpho give way.

Eddie

'Don't make me do nuttin'', he pleads with Catherine, and he threatens Rodolpho, 'Just get outa here and don't lay another hand on her unless you wanna go out feet first'. However, everything the pair have said to him makes it clear that they do not accept his demands (for Catherine to stay and Rodolpho to go) and his threats merely strengthen their resolve.

Love

We are now moving rapidly towards action; the symbolic acts are now more explicit and violent (the two kisses are accompanied by real, if brief, fighting) and not one line of dialogue is wasted. Arthur Miller does not concern himself with wrong conclusions or feeble excuses; it is obvious what is going on (both enter from the bedroom, Catherine adjusting her dress), neither denies it and the scene begins with 'Get your stuff and get outa here'.

Catherine

What Miller is interested in is not the evidence for dismissing Rodolpho, but the reaction to that dismissal.

Actions and reactions: attack and counter-attack

Let us examine Catherine first. Immediately she says that she will have to leave as well; note that she *has* to leave, not that she *wants* to. What does this show us about her feelings, both for Eddie and for Rodolpho? Then, in the speech beginning 'I think I can't stay here no more', she repeats the same ideas several times. Examine this speech (including the stage directions) and decide what Catherine feels for Eddie at this point.

Family

There is Catherine's reaction. Eddie must respond to that. He does so instantly by kissing her. There are many reasons you could think of for his kissing her at this point (the whisky he has drunk, for one thing), but it also has the symbolic force of saying, 'You ain't goin' nowheres' in action, not words.

Rodolpho

Now Rodolpho must react, and this is equally sudden: the clear statement, 'She'll be my wife', followed by an attack on Eddie which he knows to be hopeless, but which is unavoidable after Eddie's taunting. Rodolpho must fight Eddie to prove his manhood.

Honour

Why does Eddie choose to pin Rodolpho's arms and then kiss him, instead of seizing the opportunity to beat him up? Is it to prove a point to Catherine about Rodolpho? Instead it proves a point to Catherine about Eddie. Not only the words ('I'll kill you!') but the descriptions of her actions and reactions, tell us that a window onto Eddie's motives has opened for Catherine.

And where does that leave the contestants: Catherine horrified, Eddie torn between laughter and tears, Rodolpho rigid? Consider the stage directions: 'like animals that have torn at one another and broken up without a decision'. So the intended humiliation of Rodolpho has not come off: why not?

Terms are stated on both sides, threats are made by Eddie. His contempt for Rodolpho is undiminished ('Not with *that*' and calling him 'submarine' instead of his name). In his last speech he makes two threats ('feet first' and 'back in the water'). At this stage, which do we expect him to put into practice?

Dramatic impact

It is a measure of Miller's skill that we are tempted to see every scene of the play as a turning-point. And why not? He has chosen seven short periods of time in and around the Carbone house (backed up by three scenes in Alfieri's office or the prison and brief glimpses of Red Hook life) to tell a story which takes place over several months. Naturally, he chooses those that act as turning-points and he lets Alfieri tell us (where necessary) why they are important.

Even so, the opening of Act 2 provides both a major turning-point and a scene of huge dramatic impact. The four domestic scenes in Act 1 have wound up the tension, through words, symbolic gestures and body language (often detailed in the stage directions). After what you have learned in Act 1, what do you expect from Act 2? What

Chorus

we get is a much shorter act, with increasing tempo and exploding tension in two scenes of violent action: the arrest and Eddie's death. These first seven pages take us from the world of slow tension to the world of explosive action. By pages 64 and 65 discussion has been replaced by exclamation, question, broken sentences, outbursts of action and open confrontation.

Who is in the right?

That is a fair question to ask in this play, but a fair answer is harder to give. Arthur Miller succeeds in giving all his characters a point of view and some claim on audience sympathy. Since Eddie is driven by love for Catherine and wants what he sees as the best for her, you could say that he and Rodolpho are motivated in exactly the same way. However, you should consider how the actions of Eddie and Rodolpho, in particular, fix the audience's sympathies and expectations more firmly in this scene. Is it, perhaps, only now

Love

that we are convinced that Eddie is capable of anything and that the future lies with Rodolpho and Catherine? We knew there was going to be a tragedy (Alfieri told us so); do we now have a clearer idea of what form it will take?

Alfieri and Eddie: 'I want to report something. Illegal immigrants.' (pages 65–67)

December 27th: Eddie goes to Alfieri for help. Their conversation is very short, Alfieri pointing out to Eddie that he has no moral or legal right to stop Catherine marrying Rodolpho. Eddie takes the only alternative he can think of and rings the Immigration Bureau.

The key moment in the play is dealt with very briefly and in a very low-key manner. The impact of the scene depends on all that has gone before, so that the telephone call becomes an inevitable consequence. It also depends on the actor playing Eddie. He is required to convey a driven intensity (from Alfieri's description) despite being given little to say and little to do.

'I seem to tell this like a dream'

The scene can be so brief partly because of Alfieri's manner of narrating. These events are fated: he now knows why he waited so long at the office. He is unable to break the grip of fate ('almost transfixed'/'I had lost my strength'). The inevitability of tragedy is expressed in his feeling that he wants to call the police, although nothing has happened. He can hardly

Chorus   remember the conversation, so he only gives us a bit of it. What he can remember is the impression that Eddie made: the dark room, the eyes like tunnels. Before this brief scene starts, the audience knows everything: Alfieri's powerlessness, Eddie's destiny, the unreality of the whole thing, even the way Eddie should look.

Alfieri's advice

The scene is cut off at both ends. 'So in other words, he won't leave?' picks up an ongoing conversation. We are distracted from Alfieri's final words by the light rising on the telephone box – light for the next scene of the play, but also a mysterious, menacing glow. Alfieri questions perfunctorily, but we know

The law   (as he does) that the law has nothing to offer Eddie and the most important speech of Alfieri's actually spells out natural moral law: 'The law is only a word for what has a right to happen.'

The importance of family is re-stated here ('her mother'll turn over in the grave!') as is Eddie's conviction that Rodolpho 'ain't right'. Eddie is still insisting that the kissing episode shows that Rodolpho is no man; Alfieri's question, 'What did you do that for?' seems a more telling questioning of hidden motives. Mainly, though, this is a 'non-scene', deliberately so, to

Family   indicate that there is no way out.

'Give me the number of the Immigration Bureau'

The scene is again as brief as possible. With a hint of a dream, Eddie is lured towards the telephone as light rises on the booth and Alfieri's desperate, anguished calls fade into the darkness. The only extra added to the bare facts of the call is the appearance of Louis and Mike, going about their normal business: bowling again. Think about why Arthur Miller included them at this

The law   point.

Arrests and accusations (pages 67-77)

Beatrice and Catherine are preoccupied with household tasks: taking down Christmas decorations, moving the immigrants upstairs to Mrs. Dondero's. Eddie, meanwhile, is

obsessed with himself and his reputation. The wedding has been arranged for the following Saturday: Beatrice wants to make peace and Catherine is willing for Eddie to come. When Beatrice tells Eddie that the Liparis also have two immigrants staying there, Eddie panics, but it is too late: the immigration officers arrive and make four arrests. Despite Eddie's protestations, everyone knows that he is the informant. Marco spits in his face while the Liparis ignore him.

'I want my respect!'

A constant theme in these pages is Eddie's need for respect, whether from his wife or from the community. You can no doubt think of reasons why, at this time, respect is even more important to him than formerly. At first it is prompted by Beatrice's lack of attention to his continued denial that Catherine is moving out. Beatrice, dealing with a real situation, has jobs to do and is not interested in Eddie's self-centred insistence on his rights.

Honour

Love

Any talk about respect between Eddie and Beatrice has as an underlying theme his failures as a husband, his non-existent sex life. Now he states, with massive arrogance (or is it just nervous defiance?) 'I do what I feel like doin' or what I don't feel like doin' '. Though grammatically he is saying something else, the intended sense is clear enough.

Once he finds out about the other immigrants, Eddie's concern for his own reputation drives him to panic. Immediately he claims that Marco and Rodolpho might be caught in a sweep for the others ('How do you know they're not trackin' these guys?') Ironically, he betrays himself in the attempt to clear himself.

In the end, Eddie insists that Marco should apologise to him, protesting to the assembled neighbours that the accusations are false and being reduced to trying to get a nod or a word from Louis and Mike: 'He's gonna take that back'. Too late: Eddie no longer has any reputation, respect, honour or whatever word we choose. In Act 1, talking about Vinny Bolzano, Eddie told us what happens to a man who forfeits his honesty. Can you find words from there that summarise Eddie's loss of respect now?

Beatrice: 'I'm no different'

Early in this section Eddie claims that Beatrice has changed: for the worse, of course. For the last year or two (a surprisingly long period of time for him to choose) it's been 'a shootin' gallery' in the house, he says. His statements about the roles of husband and wife are full of a pathetic, self-defensive arrogance: 'I don't like. The way you talk to me and the way you look at me.'/'A wife is supposed to believe the husband.' But is Beatrice

Beatrice

different? She is certainly dismissive and off-hand, but what does she think about the family and the part that she and Eddie have to play in it now?

'They're going to get married next week'

Eddie will not attend the wedding. To begin with, he can't even talk to Catherine: he knows something they don't, of course. As for Catherine, she is willing for Eddie to attend the wedding, but hardly enthusiastic. How does Beatrice react to this unpromising position? Examine what she says about the wedding on pages 70 and 71. What does Beatrice want out of this whole sorry business? Is she seeking to lower Eddie's respect? Is she different from earlier in the play?

Family

Too late for Eddie?

Irony is a powerful weapon for both tragic and comic effect, particularly in a

play where there are so many different viewpoints. Irony operates on a basis of opposites, very often opposites between intention and achievement. Eddie's situation is ironic: he acts to keep Catherine, but drives her away; he acts to keep his good name, but destroys it. The irony is deepened by those things that he learns too late: about the Liparis' relatives, for instance,

Eddie

but also about his relationship with Catherine. What is his tone of voice for 'She asked you that?' about the wedding invitation; would Catherine's friendship have made a difference to his decision? Irony is also to be found in Beatrice's belief that Catherine still loves Eddie 'in her heart' and would welcome him if he said he was sorry. Is Eddie capable of apologising to anyone? Particularly ironic is his speech to Catherine ('I was just tellin' Beatrice...') when he belatedly sets about solving the last but two set of problems. Eddie's timing is in every way unfortunate here: his protestations that the Immigration Bureau are likely to come looking for Liparis' relatives are speedily interrupted by the men from the Bureau. What a coincidence! Almost as though he could read their minds.

'Immigration, open up'

The main effect of the arrival of the immigration men needs no explanation. Activity and movement, questions and pursuits, fury and grief all create a very dramatic scene. In production it all happens very quickly, of course, but a good director will not allow the pace to blur the details. Let us examine some of the details.

The law

The timing of the arrival

We were earlier considering irony: a particular form of this is dramatic irony, when the audience knows something which means that what a character is saying or doing is futile. Here there is a double entry for the men from Immigration. They enter the composite set (looking for the right house?) while Eddie rages about moving Marco and Rodolpho and about his sacrifices for his family. We know they are there, but there is a time-lapse before they knock on the door and ruin Eddie's attempt at escape.

The men from the Bureau

The law

Are they presented as reasonable representatives of law and order, or as the knock on the door in a Police State? There are human touches: they are called Dominick and Charley. Charley is local (he was born at 111, Union Street) and speaks a touch of Italian to them, though he translates *andiamo* for our benefit. Is their response to Catherine's protestations human or soulless? It is worth noticing the 'last informative look' that the first officer gives Eddie after he has broken up the scuffle between him and Marco.

The victims

We have already seen that Eddie's main concern is to maintain his reputation: he can see a situation where, at best, an entire neighbourhood will ignore him.

Beatrice

At worst, he will be involved in two blood feuds (one with Marco and Rodolpho, one with the Liparis), with nobody on his side. The reactions of the others share a general grief, but are not exactly the same.

Eddie's terror betrays his dark secret to Beatrice. Her horrified disbelief can express itself only in calling on God.

Catherine

Catherine bolts from the room when the officers arrive (why?) with a 'sob of fury'. Now compare the behaviour of Beatrice and Catherine when the officers bring down the immigrants. Which one is more aggressive? What is each trying to do? Compare the sentences that each of them repeats.

Marco

Marco's two rushes at Eddie, to spit at him and to point at him as a murderer, are the most striking happenings in the scene, but it is also worth looking at the words that Marco uses: in his disgust, he is quite unable to name Eddie (he becomes 'that one') and even in his fury Marco remains the family man everyone admired so much in Act 2: it is for his children that Marco curses Eddie.

Rodolpho

Rodolpho is passive: he does not argue against arrest. Why not? There are at least three possible reasons: one is that he is simply preoccupied with reassuring Catherine. What are the others?

Alfieri is not the only choric figure. The people of the neighbourhood also serve to reflect public opinion and tell us what to think. The Liparis make symbolic gestures: keening (wailing, as for the dead), kissing their relatives, turning from Eddie. Neither they nor Louis and Mike speak, but that is what is important. We must notice the fact that they do not speak.

Chorus

Self-test questions (on pages 59–77)

Uncover the plot
Delete two of the three alternatives given, to find the correct plot. Beware possible misconceptions and muddles.

On Christmas Eve/ Christmas Day/December 23rd a case of whisky/coffee/brandy slips from a net on Pier 41. Catherine asks Rodolpho about living in Eddie's house/Italy/the upstairs apartment. Rodolpho tells her of the lack of scenery/fountains/work. Catherine expresses her hatred/contempt/fondness for Eddie, who now returns drunk/tired/happy. The young couple are in the bedroom/kitchen/living room when he enters and he tells Rodolpho to leave. In a confrontation Eddie hits/laughs at/kisses both Catherine and Rodolpho. After a conversation with Alfieri proves helpful/violent/useless, Eddie telephones the Immigration Bureau.

Beatrice and Catherine have decided to move the immigrants to Mrs Donero's/hide them/send them away. When Eddie hears that other immigrants are with them, he is pleased/unconcerned/terrified at the emergence of good company/his own guilt/more Italians. The immigration officers arrest Eddie/Marco and Rodolpho/all four immigrants in a dramatic scene in which Marco/Rodolpho/Mr Lipari spits at Eddie and accuses him of murdering his children/his wife/his nephews.

Who? What? Why? When? Where? How?
1 Who was working at dressmaking on December 23rd?
2 What was Beatrice packing in a box when Eddie came in?
3 Why did Alfieri stay late at the office?
4 When is the wedding of Catherine and Rodolpho to be?
5 Where precisely does Eddie live?
6 How does Catherine react to Eddie kissing Rodolpho?

Who said... about whom?
1 'I don't say you must hate him.' (two people)
2 'They got a temper, that family.'
3 'He was born in Philadelphia.'
4 'I gave them the blankets off my bed.'
5 'Cause in her heart she still loves you.'
6 'I would be a criminal stealing your face.'

Open quotes
Find and complete the following:
1 'He's gonna take that back or...'
2 'Even those who understand will...'
3 'If I was a wife I would...'
4 'I want you to be my wife, and...'

5 'I kept wanting to call the police but....'
6 'Andiamo, andiamo...'

Prove it!
1 Find evidence in the text for the following statements: (a) the play is written about a community, not just a family; (b) Rodolpho is not marrying Catherine just for his passport.
2 Consider the view that the law is not the same as justice. Try to find examples of evidence on both sides.

'Only God makes justice': Marco in prison (pages 77–80)

Rodolpho, Catherine and Alfieri reason with Marco, who is unwilling to promise that he will not attack Eddie. However, the others explain the advantages: it is the only way he can obtain bail and, if bailed, he can attend Rodolpho's wedding and earn some money by working until the hearing. Marco reluctantly agrees.

This short scene is a contrast, in its stillness, with the explosive action before and after. It is simply a conversation, with minimal action, but it is nevertheless important. It shows the passage of time from the last scene and offers a brief rest from the passion and violence: to follow the arrest directly with the final scene would not work dramatically. It also reminds us, in a rather more calm way, of the essential themes of the play.

Honour and the law

As with Alfieri's scene with Eddie, this scene begins in mid-conversation. In

Honour
each case, Alfieri is asking a question which is, in some way, a repeat of one previously asked. This question is all about Marco's sense of honour. Marco wishes to be bailed; but to be bailed he must give a promise not to harm Eddie. Which is more dishonourable: to break that promise or to allow Eddie to escape? 'You're an honourable man, I will believe your promise,' says Alfieri. Now read Alfieri's words and the stage directions associated with him at the end of this scene (pages 79–80) and decide if he is still so confident. Marco, on the other hand, dwells on honour of a different kind: this promise, he says, is 'dishonourable'. Eddie has degraded his blood (meaning his family) and his brother and robbed his children.

Family
Marco sees it as his family duty to take revenge. He is not seeking financial compensation, but a restoration of family honour: like Eddie later, he deceives himself into thinking his enemy may wish to apologise. If so, this is enough: the name, the reputation, is restored.

Opposed to this is the law. Marco cannot understand America: 'In my country he would be dead now', he says. Most tellingly, he cannot understand that 'to promise not to kill is not dishonourable'. The two concepts of justice are offered in debate in simple, telling terms. Why is there no law against a

The law

man who has ruined a family? Is all the law in a book, as Alfieri says? Is justice something that can only come from God? You will find it helpful to compare this debate on the law, justice and honour with Alfieri's scenes with Eddie and, especially, with Alfieri's opening speech of the play.

A variant on Marco's views of honour (though with definite similarities) is offered by Catherine. She sees no need for him to harm Eddie, as Eddie's loss of honour (symbolised by Marco's spitting) means that he doesn't matter anyway: 'Nobody is gonna talk to him again if he lives to a hundred'.

Honour

The practical Americans

Marco cannot adjust from his old codes of honour. Rodolpho has already adjusted to 'settling for half' and, with Catherine, puts forward practical reasons for him promising not to harm Eddie: they both want him at the wedding. The opportunity to work is also mentioned, giving Alfieri the chance to confirm that the hearing is a formality: Marco will be deported. He also confirms that, after the wedding, Rodolpho 'can start to become an American': he will stay. Before the final violent scene and Alfieri's brief epitaph for Eddie, the remaining plot lines are cleared up: we already know what will happen after the play finishes. What do you think is gained by this?

'I want my name, Marco': marriage and death (pages 80–85)

Beatrice is preparing to accompany Catherine to her wedding. Eddie cannot be persuaded to join them, even when Rodolpho apologises to him for the troubles he has brought on them. Rodolpho also informs them that Marco is praying in the church before coming for Eddie. In the subsequent confrontation with Marco, Eddie is killed with the knife that he himself draws. Alfieri speaks an epitaph for Eddie in front of the assembled mourners.

Religion in *A View from the Bridge*

The characters in this play are all Roman Catholics and, though references to it are fairly infrequent, we can sense that religion is an important part of their lives. There is, for instance, the frequent use of the word 'bless' (Catherine early on says that Rodolpho 'blesses' Eddie; Eddie pleads with Catherine, saying he only 'blesses' her). The word means more than just 'love' or 'approve of'; it is calling down God's blessing to make sure all goes well. In Alfieri's scene with Marco, there is again much emphasis on God as the only source of justice.

Here the religion is more clear-cut. The church is going to bless the

wedding of Catherine and Rodolpho, but Marco is also asking for God's blessing on what to him is an honourable action. His prayer is like one before battle, or a bull-fighter in the chapel before entering the ring; it is a prayer for God's blessing in success or in death. Rodolpho, bringing the news of Marco praying, checks 'You understand?' and they do.

Honour

Who is guilty?

Eddie is guilty, that is obvious, but is Eddie *alone* guilty? Catherine, who held on to her love for him longer than seemed possible, now rounds on him in lines beginning, 'Who the hell do you think you are?'

Catherine

The violence of language is the more shocking coming from the mouth of Catherine. Eddie has no right to tell anyone anything, he is a poisonous sewer rat, he belongs with the other rubbish, he is outside the society of decent people. Beatrice's response is surprising. If Eddie belongs in the garbage, they all do, she says, because 'whatever happened we all done it'.

Family

Consider this statement. Is it true? *Are* they all to blame? Is Beatrice merely trying to calm Eddie down? Is her view distorted by her love for him? Whatever you decide, this is not a statement to be dismissed lightly.

Codes of honour

Beatrice's decision to stay with Eddie, despite her wish to attend the wedding, immediately becomes irrelevant, with the news of Marco's arrival. But with Rodolpho comes an apology (justified or not?) and someone else willing to share the blame.

Rodolpho

Rodolpho's behaviour at this point is remarkable. He wishes to apologise for failing to ask permission for Catherine and for bringing all the troubles, but he is not without pride. He states that Eddie insulted him, too, but he does not require an apology. He is willing to forgive: 'Maybe God understand

Honour

why you did that to me'. All that matters now is comradeship, symbolised by the kissing of the hand, which Eddie does not accept.

Rodolpho's conduct is the opposite of the code of honour which is currently driving Marco and Eddie, an explicit rejection of the blood feud. Which do you find the more honourable? Is there a place for forgiveness?

Marco

Marco kills a man after refusing to follow the reasonable arguments of Alfieri,

Marco

Catherine and Rodolpho. He has gone back on his word to Alfieri. Does that make him a villain? It is certainly hard to accept Marco as a villain: even Eddie, we are reminded, 'always liked Marco'. Arthur Miller does not tell us that Marco is found guilty of murder; quite possibly, he is merely deported, as would have happened anyway. But look at the methods Miller uses to blur Marco's guilt. Almost his last words with Alfieri are 'Maybe he wants to apologise to me', so perhaps that is why he is coming to see Eddie. So why go to church first? Maybe he fears Eddie will provoke a fatal struggle. Not very convincing, but enough to blur our certainty... and what do you think would have been Marco's reaction to an apology?

When he arrives, he speaks only once (to call 'Eddie Carbone!' – the name, symbol of respect and honour) and no indication is given of his aggressive mood or actions until Eddie moves for him. Then, calling Eddie an animal, he strikes him down: again, the symbolism is all-important – Eddie on his knees to Marco. The lethal knife, of course, comes from Eddie. Just how guilty is Marco? You would be naive to think that he was coming to have a pre-wedding chat with Eddie, but there are levels of guilt and layers of honour.

'The truth is not as bad as blood'

There is a double climax to the play: truth and blood. On page 83 the two follow in immediate sequence. Beatrice finally says, 'You want somethin' else, Eddie, and you can never have her!' Catherine is horrified, Eddie is described as shocked, horrified, agonised, crying out, clenching his bursting head, refusing to believe that Beatrice would think that of him. And then Marco calls his name.

So we need to find our way through the double climax of truth and blood

Eddie

by examining Eddie's words and actions. To begin with, he is doggedly convinced that he is in the right: Marco must apologise to him. If Beatrice goes to the wedding, she need not come back; they are either on his side or against him. He responds to Catherine's insults by nearly throwing the table at her: what does that suggest about his state of mind? Eddie will

Honour

not respond to the news of Marco or to Rodolpho's apology. The reason Eddie gives is that he wants his name. Rodolpho is only a kid, a punk. What he does is of no account; only Marco can give him his name back and, if he doesn't, 'we have it out'. But now we have to question his motives: Beatrice says that Marco has nothing to give him. What he really wants is Catherine.

Love

This may well be the truth, but it invites many other questions:

Is the person Eddie needs to get his 'name' from really himself? Does he refuse to accept any peace-making because his real lack of peace is within himself?

Does he now realise that he is doomed, and resolve on a desperate last act?

Certainly Eddie now presents himself like the doomed protagonist in a tragedy. If you have read or seen *Macbeth*, this last scene may remind you of Macbeth being so weighed down by his sins, and the desertion of friends and followers, that he goes recklessly to his death. Eddie goes out of the house and addresses 'the people'. Again, the community suggests the background of normal-thinking people.

Chorus

In his speech, 'Maybe he come to apologise to me…', Eddie gradually makes himself angry ('incensing himself') as he argues his version of events to the people of Red Hook. If they do not accept that he is right, he cannot live among them, so Marco is accused three times of lying and told (also three times) to admit it, or give Eddie his name (the same thing). Every stage of the fight is provoked by Eddie, but his death comes swiftly. Both women support his body and call his name, but notice whose name *Eddie* calls, who protects his dead body in her arms.

Love

As Eddie dies, reflect upon what that final act of love tells us about the tragedy. Reflect also on the significance (for the drama, for the character) of Catherine's last line.

Alfieri's epitaph for Eddie

Chorus

In this scene, we are taken back to the beginning: compare the words of Alfieri now and then. Eddie is finally the subject of the tragedy – not that he is the most heroic or sympathetic figure in the play, but he is the one with whose character and dilemma the audience has most fully identified, the one whose force has driven the tragedy. Arthur Miller records that, when the play was first shown, many audience members identified to such an extent that they were convinced they knew the original 'Eddie Carbone' – many different people, needless to say! Alfieri's words are the equivalent of a funeral sermon, but they leave questions, not certainties. Why, in particular, does Alfieri feel as he does? He trembles and mourns Eddie with a certain alarm. He loves him more than his other clients, but finds him wrong and thinks that he should have settled for half. Why does Alfieri have these contradictions? Do you share them?

A view from *which* bridge?

It is always interesting to think why playwrights choose the names they do for their plays. For instance, you may have noticed that all Shakespeare's tragedies have the name(s) of one or two tragic protagonists in their titles, while the comedies tell us what fun we are going to have: *As You Like It, Much Ado about Nothing, A Comedy of Errors* and so on. He is telling us what is important in the different types of play. So this play could have been called *The Tragedy of Eduardo Carbone*. Why, then, is it called *A View from the Bridge*?

Literally, the play is, of course, set in the shadow of Brooklyn Bridge and is about the community there, not just Eddie's family. Now try to think of some hidden meanings:

For what is a bridge a metaphor?

Whose view is a bridge between Old World and New, old life and new?

In what ways can the community be seen as a bridge?

If there is a bridge, to where (at the end of the play) is it crossing?

Self-test questions (on pages 77–85)

Uncover the plot

Delete two of the three alternatives given, to find the correct plot. Beware possible misconceptions and muddles.

Marco is in prison/at Alfieri's office/at the Immigration Bureau. Alfieri wants the answer to one question: will he promise not to harm Eddie? Marco thinks that to let Eddie live is honourable/dishonourable/easy. Rodolpho and Catherine try to persuade him so that he can attend their party/house-warming/wedding. Marco feels that he must protect/avenge/ignore his family. Eventually he agrees: Alfieri is delighted/shocked/doubtful at his promise. At the house, Eddie is refusing to let Beatrice/Catherine/Rodolpho go to the wedding, even when Catherine/Marco/Rodolpho apologises to him. Beatrice finally accuses him of wanting not an apology, but a feud/a fight/Catherine. At this moment Marco arrives and Eddie/Marco/Catherine makes a long, self-justifying speech before the crowd. Beatrice, Catherine and Rodolpho strive to encourage/restrain/defeat Eddie. In the fight, Marco/Eddie/Rodolpho draws a knife. The scene of Eddie's death reveals his love/neglect/contempt for Beatrice. Alfieri's epitaph respects something pure/fierce/sensible in Eddie.

Who? What? Why? When? Where? How?

1 Who tried to break up the fight until threatened with a knife?
2 What did Rodolpho do to symbolise his apology to Eddie?
3 Why did Alfieri require a promise from Marco?
4 When will Marco's tribunal be?
5 Where did Marco go before he went to Eddie's house?
6 How much chance does Marco have of remaining in America?

Who said... about whom?

1 'If he obeys the law, he lives.'
2 'And so I mourn him – I admit it – with a certain... alarm.'
3 'It was wrong that I did not ask your permission.'
4 'He can't bail you out if you're gonna do something bad.' (two people)
5 'He bites people when they sleep.'
6 'Which he said I killed his children!'

Open quotes

Find and complete the following:

1 'You're an honourable man...'
2 'To come out of the water and...'
3 '...not purely good but...'
4 'Now gimme my name and...'
5 'To promise not to kill...'
6 'Eddie, I never meant to...'

Prove it!

1 Find evidence in this last part of the play to prove the importance of family to the characters.
2 What evidence is there that Marco intends a violent confrontation with Eddie? Is there any evidence to suggest that this is *not* his intention?
3 Explain what the implications of 'blood' are, using evidence from this section.

■ About Arthur Miller

When Arthur Miller's autobiography, *Timebends*, was first published in 1987, much of the press comment was directed to his account of his troubled married life with the doomed film star, Marilyn Monroe. In fact, *Timebends* was speedily recognised as one of the finest accounts of an author's life. As a student of Arthur Miller's plays, you should make sure that your school/college/public library has a copy and at least sample it, with the aid of the index.

Arthur Miller, born in New York in 1915, is still active in theatre today. New plays by him, such as *The Last Yankee* (1992) and *Broken Glass* (1994), have been recently staged in London and elsewhere in Britain, as well as numerous revivals of *A View from the Bridge, Death of a Salesman*, etc. In 1996, the Royal Exchange in Manchester even produced a version of *The Misfits*, the film script he wrote for Marilyn Monroe.

Arthur Miller is a first-generation American, his father having emigrated from Poland as a child. Suffering, like many Americans, from the Great Depression of the 1930s, Miller worked his way through college. Although he began writing plays then, he had to wait for the post-war years for his first successes.

By then, his experiences in the depression years and his awareness of the horrors of fascism in Europe had led him towards communism. Although he was no longer a member of the party by that time, he still held left-wing views which are obvious throughout the great quartet of plays that made his reputation. As well as displaying a sympathy towards 'ordinary' people, these plays (all of tragic impact, ending with the deaths of their protagonists) dwell on the need for personal integrity.

Three are set in the present day of the time. *All My Sons* (1947) searched the conscience of an industrialist who had caused the deaths of American airmen in World War Two by supplying faulty parts. *Death of a Salesman* (1949) explored the broken world of an ageing salesman whose dreams are shattered. *A View from the Bridge* appeared in 1955. *The Crucible* (1953) was set in 1692, but had a major contemporary theme. Its subject of 17th century witch trials was clearly related to the 1950s purge on communists and communist sympathisers. Miller himself suffered before the House Un-American Activities Committee.

This committee, dominated by Senator Joseph McCarthy, investigated possible communists in public life. Just as with the witch-trials, the way to escape was to find someone else to implicate.

Timebends reveals Miller's personal and political views with great clarity and the background to *A View from the Bridge* comes into sharp focus. In World War Two, he spent nearly two years working in the Brooklyn Navy Yard and his descriptions of it call up the world of *A View from the Bridge*: a near-majority of Italians in the work force, elaborate treacheries, Sicilian dramas, unpredictable moral codes. Later, he investigated the life of one Pete Panto, a young longshoreman who had attempted to organise a rank-and-file revolt against the alleged Mafiosi of the International Longshoremen's Association. Panto simply 'disappeared' one night. Miller's projected film on the subject came to nothing, but this was another element making up the authenticity of *A View from the Bridge*. As a New Yorker whose father came from Europe, he was himself in the same position as Eddie and, though Poland is of course not Italy, Miller had familiarised himself with Sicilian village life by the time he wrote the play.

Many of Miller's recent plays are still extremely powerful, some showing the same willingness to confront difficult issues and make them work on stage. *Broken Glass*, for instance, is a remarkable study of the effects of Hitler's persecution of the Jews on an American Jewish family. However, for many of his admirers, his major achievement remains the four plays of 1947 to 1955, which set new standards for American realist drama.

Timebends, published in this country in 1987 by Methuen, is currently available in Minerva paperback.

Self-test answers (on pages 11–33)

Uncover the plot

The play is set in Red Hook and is introduced by Alfieri, who is a lawyer. From the beginning, he makes it clear that tragedy is inevitable. Eddie Carbone is delighted to see his niece Catherine looking so beautiful, but the news that she has found a job makes him worried. He, too, has news: his wife's cousins will arrive from Italy at ten o'clock. They are illegal immigrants, so it is important not to betray them. Eddie and Beatrice, his wife, welcome the cousins, Marco and Rodolpho, and are amazed at Rodolpho's blond hair. Marco is strong and silent, but his brother tells stories about his singing and wishes to buy a motorcycle. When he starts to sing, his voice is a high tenor. Eddie is very troubled at Catherine's attentive behaviour towards Rodolpho.

Who? What? Why? When? Where? How?

1 Vinny Bolzano (page 23)
2 Sang at the hotel (page 31)
3 Because they are on their own/because of the danger of immigration officers (page 26)
4 In four, five or six years (page 29)
5 In Nostrand Avenue by the Navy Yard (page 18)
6 Because they owe the organisation money (page 27)

Who said... about whom?

1 Marco about Rodolpho (page 31)
2 Marco about Tony, the man who brought them to Eddie's (page 27)
3 Alfieri about Al Capone (page 12)
4 Eddie about the Immigration Bureau (page 23)
5 Eddie about Catherine (page 20)
6 Rodolpho about Marco (page 29)

Open quotes

1 'And now we are quite civilised, quite American.' (page 12)
2 'The horses in our town are skinnier than goats.' (page 28)
3 '...she's seventeen years old, you gonna keep her in the house all her life?' (page 20)
4 '...you can quicker get back a million dollars that was stole than a word that you gave away.' (page 24)
5 'My wife – she feeds them from her own mouth.' (page 29)
6 'He was as good a man as he had to be in a life that was hard and even.' (page 26)

Prove it!

1 Alfieri's opening words: a lawyer is unlucky. Alfieri's description of justice: 'justly shot by unjust men' (page 12). Eddie's account of the Immigration Bureau/Vinny Bolzano (pages 22–23, also page 33). Tony and the organisation that provides work outside the law (pages 26–27). *This is not a complete list.*
2 Again, too many to list, but you should mention Vinny Bolzano (page 23), Eddie and Catherine ('Katie, I promised your mother on her deathbed' – page 14) and Beatrice and her cousins ('as soon as you see a tired relative, I end up on the floor' – page 16 – and many other examples).
3 The evidence is in Marco's reactions: for instance, living off the proceeds of singing for two months, not six (page 31), whether the English thought he was too loud (pages 31–32), 'he dreams, he dreams' (page 31).

Self-test answers (on pages 33–58)

Uncover the plot

Eddie waits for Catherine and Rodolpho to return from the cinema. He is worried about their relationship, because he regards Rodolpho as effeminate. His opinion is supported by Louis and Mike. When Catherine returns, Eddie emphasises a different concern: that Rodolpho is using her to gain his passport. Catherine then talks to Beatrice, whose advice is to behave in a more adult manner to Eddie. Beatrice encourages Catherine's relationship with Rodolpho. Eddie seeks help from Alfieri, but is told that the only concern of the law in this case is illegal immigration. Eddie is furious when Alfieri points out that Catherine cannot marry him. In the house, Catherine defies Eddie by dancing with Rodolpho. Eddie then attempts to affirm his manhood by sparring with Rodolpho, but Marco responds by successfully challenging Eddie to a trial of strength.

Who? What? Why? When? Where? How?

1 Louis and Mike (page 38)
2 Cut it up and make a new one (page 47)
3 In order not to offend Eddie: 'in deference to Eddie' (page 54)
4 When there was no work ('empty piers') in Brooklyn (page 49)
5 To a 'wise old woman' in the neighbourhood (page 50)
6 There are no fountains (page 39)

Who said... about whom?

1 Mike about Marco (page 37)
2 Alfieri about Eddie (page 45)
3 Beatrice about Catherine (page 44)
4 Eddie about Rodolpho (page 54)
5 Eddie about Rodolpho (page 49)
6 Catherine about Eddie and Rodolpho (page 40)

Open quotes

1 'Well, he ain't exackly funny, but he's always like making remarks like, y'know?' (page 37)
2 'Girls don't have to wear black dress to be strict.' (page 52)
3 '...there is too much love for the daughter, there is too much love for the niece.' (page 48)
4 'But if you act like a baby and he be treatin' you like a baby.' (page 43)
5 'And with that wacky hair; he's like a chorus girl or sump'm.' (page 35)
6 'It's almost three months you don't feel good...' (page 36)

Prove it!

1 Marco 'goes around like a man; nobody kids Marco' (page 35); 'a strong guy' (page 37); 'we go to the bouts next Saturday night' (page 55).
   Rodolpho 'like a chorus girl' and 'I just hope that's his regular hair' (both page 35); 'the guy ain't right' (page 46); 'you be lookin' for her', 'like an angel', 'so sweet', "Paper Doll" they call him' (all page 47); he should be in a 'dress store' (page 55). *This is not a complete list.*
2 Mainly on pages 50-52. 'If they catch fish they pay all right'; nobody in Marco's family owned a boat; 'yiz all starvin'; Marco's wife can get medicine for the child only now he is working in the USA; fathers who have to work away permanently.

3 Pages 45-49: 'There's nothing illegal about a girl falling in love with an immigrant.' 'Even if you could prove that – (the first of several interrupted speeches beginning 'Yes, but that's not' – or something similar). 'I don't get you' and questions showing lack of comprehension. 'The law is very specific'. 'You have no recourse in the law.' 'The law is not interested in this.' Alfieri also says, 'There's only one legal question here', but that is not what Eddie has come to him for.

Self-test answers (on pages 59–77)

Uncover the plot
On December 23rd a case of whisky slips from a net on Pier 41. Catherine asks Rodolpho about living in Italy. Rodolpho tells her of the lack of work. Catherine expresses her fondness for Eddie, who now returns drunk. The young couple are in the bedroom when he enters and he tells Rodolpho to leave. In a confrontation Eddie kisses both Catherine and Rodolpho. After a conversation with Alfieri proves useless, Eddie telephones the Immigration Bureau.
Beatrice and Catherine have decided to move the immigrants to Mrs. Dondero's. When Eddie hears that other immigrants are with them, he is terrified at the emergence of his own guilt. The immigration officers arrest all four immigrants in a dramatic scene in which Marco spits at Eddie and accuses him of murdering his children.

Who? What? Why? When? Where? How?
1 Catherine (page 59)
2 Christmas decorations (page 67)
3 Because he 'knew' Eddie would come, as he was fated to (page 65)
4 Next week (page 70) or on Saturday (page 71)
5 441, Saxon Street, Brooklyn (page 67)
6 By attacking Eddie, tearing at his face/by threatening to kill him (page 64)

Who said... about whom?
1 Rodolpho about Catherine and Eddie (page 63)
2 Eddie about the Liparis (page 73)
3 Catherine about Rodolpho (page 75)
4 Eddie about Marco and Rodolpho (page 77)
5 Beatrice about Catherine and Eddie (page 70)
6 Rodolpho about Catherine (page 60)

Open quotes
1 'He's gonna take that back or I'll kill him.' (page 77)
2 'Even those who understand will turn against you.' (page 67)
3 'If I was a wife I would make a man happy instead of goin' at him all the time.' (page 62)
4 'I want you to be my wife, and I want to be a citizen.' (page 61)
5 'I kept wanting to call the police, but nothing had happened.' (page 65)
6 '*Andiamo, andiamo*, let's go.' (page 75)

Prove it!
1 (a) You might find evidence of the community working together to get the whisky (page 59) and the appearance of Louis and Mike (page 67) is a reminder, but the main examples are co-operation between Beatrice and

Mrs. Dondero and the Liparis (pages 67 and 72) and the reactions at the arrests: community solidarity, rejection of Eddie (pages 76-77).

(b) Part of the evidence is the love they show for each other (pages 62-63 in particular), but a specific point is that Rodolpho does not take the chance to lie to impress Eddie (page 62) and speaks so honestly about poverty, work, etc. (pages 60-61).

2 The whole immigration business is simply a set of rules: it's unjust that Marco has to go back and starve. The community sees the law as outside themselves. Alfieri says the law can be unnatural (page 66). On the other hand, he makes clear that the law's failure to help Eddie is perfectly natural. Also, the immigration officers only act in response to Eddie's call and do not seem like the representatives of an alien Police State (page 73 onwards).

Self-test answers (on pages 77–85)

Uncover the plot

Marco is in prison. Alfieri wants the answer to one question: will he promise not to harm Eddie? Marco thinks that to let Eddie live is dishonourable. Rodolpho and Catherine try to persuade him so that he can attend their wedding. Marco feels that he must avenge his family. Eventually he agrees: Alfieri is doubtful at his promise. At the house, Eddie is refusing to let Beatrice go to the wedding, even when Rodolpho apologises to him. Beatrice finally accuses him of wanting not an apology, but Catherine. At this moment Marco arrives and Eddie makes a long, self-justifying speech before the crowd. Beatrice, Catherine and Rodolpho strive to restrain Eddie. In the fight, Eddie draws a knife. The scene of Eddie's death reveals his love for Beatrice. Alfieri's epitaph respects something pure in Eddie.

Who? What? Why? When? Where? How?

1 Louis (page 84)
2 Tried to kiss his hand (page 82)
3 To obtain bail (page 78)
4 In five or six weeks (page 79)
5 To church (page 81)
6 None: the hearing is a formality (page 78)

Who said... about whom?

1 Alfieri about Eddie (page 79)
2 Alfieri about Eddie again (page 85)
3 Rodolpho about Eddie (page 82)
4. Catherine about Alfieri and Marco (page 78)
5 Catherine about Eddie (page 81)
6 Eddie about Marco (page 82)

Open quotes

1 'You're an honourable man, I will believe your promise.' (page 78)
2 'To come out of the water and grab a girl for a passport?' (page 83)
3 '...not purely good, but himself purely.' (page 85)
4 'Now gimme my name and we go together to the wedding.' (page 84)
5 'To promise not to kill is not dishonourable.' (page 78)
6 'Eddie, I never meant to do nothing bad to you.' (page 84)

Prove it!

1   'How can I be married and you're in here?', says Rodolpho to his brother (page 78) and Beatrice has a similar concern (page 80). Marco stresses his argument with Eddie is over brother and children (page 79). Beatrice accepts that the whole family is to blame (page 81). On page 83, family is both the reason to fight (Marco and Eddie – 'to go and take from your own family like from the stable') and to make peace ('Eddie, please, he has children').

2   He tells Alfieri it is (pages 78-79) but we, perhaps, doubt his promise. He prays in church (page 81). He calls Eddie out (page 83). He speaks no words of peace and strikes a fighting posture (page 84). There is no evidence to suggest that it is not, but some to reduce certainty. He says nothing until Eddie attacks, except for the name, which Eddie treats as a challenge. He has made a promise. Eddie makes every first move.

3   'Blood' is blood, as in family, as in feud, as in purification. 'Only blood is good' (page 82) is shedding blood, but when Marco says 'My blood' (page 79), he means family. Of course, bloodshed and blood (family) come together in the blood-feud.

■ Writing an examination essay

Take the following to heart

- *Carefully study each of the questions set on a particular text* Make sure you understand what they are asking for so that you select the one you know most about.
- *Answer the question* Obvious, isn't it? But bitter experience shows that many students fail because they do not actually answer the question that has been set.
- *Answer all the question* Again, obvious, but so many students spend all their time answering just part of a question and ignoring the rest. This prevents you gaining marks for the parts left out.

The question

1 Read and understand every word of it. If it asks you to compare (the similarities) and/or contrast (the differences) between characters or events, then that is what you must do.
2 Underline all the key words and phrases that mention characters, events and themes, and all instructions as to what to do, e.g. compare, contrast, outline, comment, give an account, write about, show how/what/where.
3 Now write a short list of the things you have to do, one item under the other. A typical question will only have between two and five items at most for you to cope with.

Planning your answer

1 Look at each of the points you have identified from the question. Think about what you are going to say about each. Much of it will be pretty obvious, but if you think of any good ideas, jot them down before you forget them.
2 Decide in what order you are going to deal with the question's major points. Number them in sequence.
3 So far you have done some concentrated, thoughtful reading and written down maybe fifteen to twenty words. You know roughly what you are going to say in response to the question and in what order – if you do not, you have time to give serious thought to trying one of the other questions.

Putting pen to paper

The first sentences are important. Try to summarise your response to the question so the examiner has some idea of how you are going to approach it. Do not say 'I am going to write about the character of Macbeth and show how evil he was' but instead write 'Macbeth was a weak-willed, vicious traitor. Totally dominated by his "fiend-like queen", he deserved the epitaph "this dead butcher" – or did he?' Jump straight into the essay, do not nibble at its extremities for a page and a half. High marks will be gained by the candidate who can show he or she has a mind engaged with the text. Your personal response is rewarded – provided you are answering the question!

As you write your essay *constantly refer back to your list of points* and make sure you are actually responding to them.

How long should it be?

There is no 'correct' length. What you must do is answer the question set, fully and sensitively, in the time allowed. Allocate time to each question according to the percentage of marks awarded for it.

How much quotation or paraphrase?

Use only that which is relevant and contributes to the quality and clarity of your answer. Padding is a waste of your time and gains not a single mark.